# 'twas the night before
## the **REAL**
# Christmas

*by Glenda Owens*

*Illustrated by Ty Schafrath*

*Twas the night before the REAL Christmas*
by Glenda Owens
Illustrated by Ty Schafrath

Printed in the United States of America

ISBN 9781498407809

Registration Number TXu 1-889-007
effective date of registration: November 26, 2013

www.xulonpress.com

# DEDICATION

I Dedicate this book to
- My Savior and Lord Jesus Christ -
who is the REAL author of this book!

- To my Grandchildren whom I love very much -
Charis the prettiest, sweetest & smartest girl on earth
who calls me "MiMi"
and
Caleb who after living on this earth for 100 hours is
very much alive in our hearts & with Jesus in Heaven!

- To my Family and Friends -
Thank you for your wonderful encouragement & support!

- To Ty Schafrath -
The kindest, most patient and talented artist!
Your illustrations are truly blessings from above

Charis and Caleb it's time for us to read
"Twas the Night Before the REAL Christmas!"

There wasn't a place to be found,
For them to lay their heads down.

Mary and Joseph expecting their first child,
Traveled far together for quite a long while.

The road was so dusty and bumpy,
And the donkey so stinky and lumpy,
That all Mary wanted
Was a place to get rested.

When suddenly there before them stood,
A humble stable all made of wood.

A donkey, a cow, some chicken and sheep,
Seemed to greet them with joy as they moved in to sleep.

For tonight is a special night as Mary already knew,
God's son, baby Jesus is born for me and you.
As she wrapped Him snuggly in very soft cloth,
And laid Him ever so carefully in a feeding trough,

The stars up above so vast and bright,
Seemed to twinkle and dance as they gave them their light.
The animals moved close to take their first peek,
As precious baby Jesus gave his first squeak!

13

On this first Christmas night such awe and wonder,
Gave Mary laughter and joy to think and ponder.

The scene for all was one of love,
As God's only son came down from above.

15

Where out in the fields, Shepherds watching over their sheep,
Awoke from their sleep and gave a great leap!
For there stood an Angel all dressed in white,
But all they could do was bow in fright!

The glory of the Lord shone around them and they were terrified!
"Fear Not, Fear Not" the Angel said to clarify!
Today a Savior has been born in a stable,
Jesus our Lord to forgive sin is able.

The Shepherds spoke not a word,
For they knew what to do from what they had heard.
To Bethlehem they traveled far that night,
The Star led the way to give them light.

One by one they came and stood,
Bowed down before baby Jesus as all should.

His eyes how they smiled, a round little nose,
His cheeks were so chubby, with soft fingers and toes.

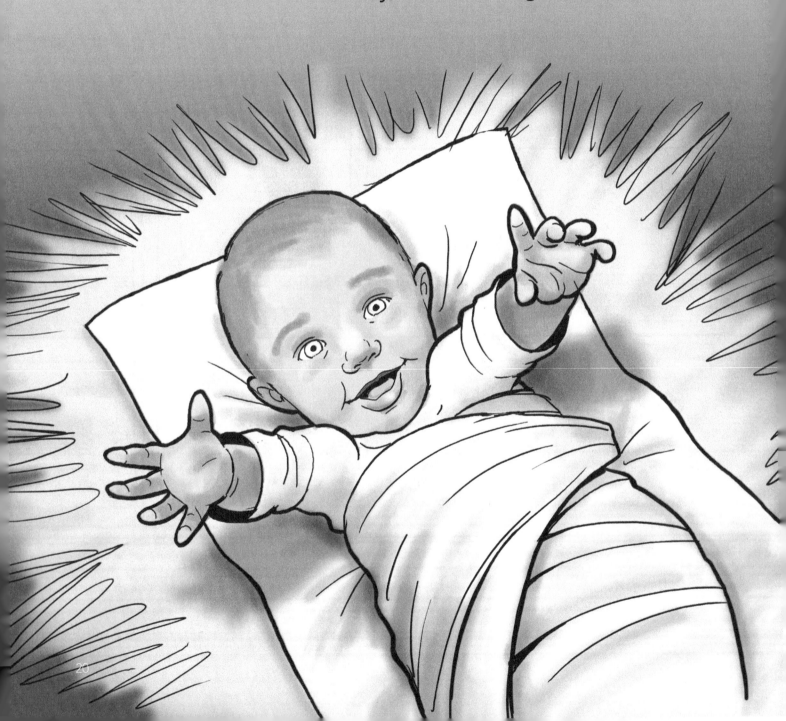

This sweet baby asleep on the hay,
Has come down from Heaven to show us the way.
The animals and Shepherds, Mary and Joseph all see,
This child has been born to set us free.

So come to the stable and see for yourself,
This child born to bring us such wealth.

Heaven He offers to one and all,
If we will but only heed His call.

Accept Jesus as your Savior and receive,
The love and forgiveness He offers to all who believe.
This Christmas night is surely one of wonder,

25

*So children everywhere always remember!*
*Every Christmas our gifts we bring,*
*Are to Jesus Christ our Lord and King.*

# You are Special To God!

**God Loves You!** The Bible says, "For God so Loved the world, that He gave His only Son, that whoever believes in Him should not perish but have eternal life." (John 3:16) ESV

*God loves you so much that He sent His one and only Son, Jesus Christ*

**God Loves You but Sin separates us from God.** The Bible says, " For all have sinned and fall short of the glory of God" (Romans 3:23) and " For the wages of sin is death, but the free gift of God is eternal life in Christ Jesus our Lord." (Romans 6:23) ESV

*God loves us to much to leave us in our sins*

**God Showed His Love for you** The Bible says, " but God shows his love for us in that while we were still sinners, Christ died for us."(Romans 5:8) ESV

*God sent Jesus Christ His Son to die on the cross for*
*our sins and take the punishment we deserve*

**God wants you to accept Jesus as your Savior.** Jesus said to him, "I am the way, and the truth, and the life. No one comes to the Father except through me." (John 14:6) and "For everyone who calls on the name of the Lord will be saved." (Romans 10:13) ESV

## Accept Jesus as Your Savior today!

 Admit you are a sinner

 Believe in Jesus

 Confess Jesus as Savior

### *See you in Heaven!*

CPSIA information can be obtained at www.ICGtesting.com
Printed in the USA
BVOW10*0723191114

375773BV00004B/7/P